At the Heart of

Friendship

Kathy Collard Miller

ACCENT PUBLICATIONS
Colorado Springs, Colorado

Daughters of the King Bible Study Series

Choices of the Heart
Contentment
Character of the King
My Father in Me
Whispers of My Heart
Romantic Love—My Father's Gift
Celebrating the Heart of Marriage
Women with Courageous Hearts
Let Every Mother Rejoice
Shadows of Sovereignty
At the Heart of Friendship
Heart Wisdom

Accent Publications
P.O. Box 36640
4050 Lee Vance View
Colorado Springs, Colorado 80918

Copyright © 1999 Accent Publications
Printed in the United States of America

Library of Congress Catalog Card Number 95-77962
ISBN 0-7814-5555-3

Contents

"So shall the king greatly desire thy beauty: for he is thy lord; and worship thou him. . . . The king's daughter is all glorious within: her clothing is of wrought gold."

Psalm 45:11,13

Rejoicing Together

*F*riendships among women are a wonderful gift from God—
especially when those friendships are relationships which have
God at the center. Although not every friendship in your life will be
this way, a friendship in the Lord is cause for rejoicing.

1. How do you define "friendship"?

What do you look for most in a friend?

2. Read Luke 1:26-56. Although Mary and Elizabeth are
relatives, what lets you know they are also friends?

3. What positive characteristic(s) of a friendship do you see in
their relationship?

4. Sometimes it is difficult to rejoice with a friend's good news. Why do you think people, even Christians, have trouble with that at times?

What do you learn from Elizabeth's good example?

5. What does Romans 12:15 command?

How do you think that can be done best?

Why do you think God gave us these two commands?

How do you prefer that people rejoice with you?

When they do, how does that make you feel?

6. What do the following verses from Proverbs say are some of the possible results when we encourage someone?

- 12:25—

- 15:13—

- 15:15—

- 15:30—

- 17:22—

How does Proverbs 27:9 describe a good friend?

What personal characteristics does this description suggest and how can you be an example of those in your friendships?

7. What warning does Proverbs 27:14 give when sharing joy?

Are there any other conditions or circumstances you think would govern "when" we share our happiness? Why?

How would you apply these truths in a practical way in your friendships?

8. An important part of sharing joy and love in a friendship is assuring your friend that you are praying for that person. Pick someone who is important to you (other than a husband or child) and pray the following verses for her. What is the essential truth of each verse? What are you asking God to do for your friend?

Ephesians 1:18-19—
   truth:
   prayer:
Ephesians 3:14-20—
   truth:
   prayer:
Philippians 1:9-11—
   truth:
   prayer:
Colossians 1:9-14—
   truth:
   prayer:
Colossians 2:6-7—
   truth:
   prayer:

Choose one of these passages and write it in your own words as a prayer for your friend. Send it to her as a note of joy and encouragement.

9. What does I John 3:18 encourage us to do in our friendships?

Has God been encouraging you to do something for a friend, and yet you've delayed? What does your friend need that you can help her with?

10. Read James 2:15-24. Why was Abraham called God's friend?

Would God say that about your friendship with Him?

How would others—perhaps friends you haven't met yet—know you are a friend of God?

How can you cultivate and develop your friendship with God?

11. How can you apply the truths you've studied in these passages in your friendships?

How will you rejoice together with a friend this week?

How do you make new friends?

Who will you approach in the next two weeks with the purpose of making her into a friend?

My Precious Princess and Daughter—

I am the Creator of heaven, earth—and your friendships. My desire is that your friends will be a blessing to you and represent the best of a relationship with Me, your very best Friend. It is My heart's desire that you will do that for them, too.

I've uniquely designed the godly friendships that women have with other women. I've made you to value relationships. Your heart's urge to reach out to others is a reflection of My heart's desire.

There are so many women who need your friendship. I have so much joy to give you through others. Won't you open up your circle of friends and make room for more of this wonderful gift? You are special, and I know how much you have to give. That doesn't mean there won't be problems, Dear One, but I will bless you through your friendships with other women.

Although a human friendship cannot give you the joy that My friendship can, I use friendships in your life to help meet many of your needs. But only I can completely fulfill that need inside you for intimacy and interaction with another person. So enjoy your friendships as one of My gifts to you, but remember that they are inadequate and incomplete in comparison to My love for you. When you're seeking friendships, will you seek Mine first?

I'm eager to reveal more of Myself to you—and to your friends through you.

Lovingly,
Your Heavenly Father, the King

Resisting Envy

*S*ometimes friendships go through difficult times—even with the best of friends. One thing that creates pain and damages any relationship is envy. Rejoicing with a friend and envying a friend are mutually exclusive. Our God will help us overcome that friendship-destroyer.

1. What areas offer the potential for envy between friends?

Have you ever observed or identified how such negative feelings begin? What causes or triggers envy?

2. What destructive consequences of envy have you observed?

3. Read I Samuel 1:1-28. Describe the reason for Hannah's envy in this situation.

How did Elkanah try to help the situation (1:8)?

Why do you think Hannah wasn't comforted by his efforts?

Although the circumstances may have been different, have you ever felt like Hannah? What triggered your feelings? How did you overcome them?

4. How did Hannah respond negatively to this situation (1:7,10)?

How did she respond positively (1:10-11)?

How and why was she rewarded (1:18-20)?

5. Obviously Penninah was a very poor friend. What do you think motivated her negative behavior toward Hannah?

What, if anything, could have made them friends?
Have you ever acted like Penninah (1:6-7)? Why would we do this to someone?

How can such attitudes be changed and controlled?

6. Read Romans 12:9-21. From each verse, give ways to resist envy.

- 12:9—

- 12:10-11—

- 12:12-13—

- 12:14—

- 12:15—

- 12:16—

- 12:17-21—

7. What ways to fight envy does I Corinthians 3:4-9 offer?

In any kind of ministry, what kinds of envy can surface?

How will this passage from I Corinthians help you keep a godly attitude?

8. What truth does Proverbs 14:30 teach about the results of envy or jealousy?

What is the opposite of envy as described in this verse?

How will you cultivate such a heart?

9. Read Proverbs 23:15-18. Who might Christians be tempted to envy whether they are friends or enemies?

Why might God have linked a wise heart and our speech to the command in 23:17?

Why do you think Christians sometimes envy sinners?

Why does Proverbs 24:1-2,19-20 say not to envy evil people?

10. Read Proverbs 18:8. How do you think envy and gossip are related?

When you feel envious of someone, are you more tempted to gossip about that person? If so, why?

How will you resist that temptation next time?

11. How could obeying Colossians 3:8 help a person who is prone to envy?

Which of the things listed in Colossians 3:8 do you need to work on the most?

How will you do that this week?

How will that help you specifically with envy?

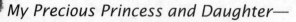

My Precious Princess and Daughter—

I understand the temptation of envy, and I realize the challenge that you face to resist it. I want you to use My strength to overcome envy's pull in your life. If you focus on others, instead of on My great love for you, it will be easy to think they are getting something or someone you don't have. But, My Beloved Child, I know what is best for you. Will you believe that I know exactly what you need?

It may seem at times that life isn't fair and that you're not getting what you deserve. Other women may have more possessions, greater outward beauty, or the kind of ministry you want. You could even envy a woman for her husband. Or, like Hannah, you may want to have children, and I haven't provided the fulfillment of that desire.

When those envious or jealous feelings well up inside you, use My strength to keep from acting on them. Resist those feelings by reflecting on My abundant provision for you. Even when things seem to be missing in your life, trust that I will work all things out for the best. I promise that you will always have everything necessary to help you be the godly woman I want you to be.

You are My chosen daughter, and you need never feel envious toward your friends or those who don't know Me. Keep your eyes on Me, the lover of your soul. Don't let our enemy, Satan, influence you to harbor feelings that deny My presence in your life. Turn your attention to Me; I love you so much. I am your Father. There is nothing to envy in others.

Lovingly,
Your Heavenly Father, the King

Friends in Marriage

s your husband your friend? Friendship in marriage is the best kind of friendship. Sadly, it is also where being friends can be the toughest challenge. Perhaps you are not married; take this opportunity to learn from the experience of others. God has given women unique perspectives and insights they can share with each other. Love, marriage, and friendship—they can go together.

1. If a married couple are the best of friends, what qualities do you think characterize their relationship?

Do you have those characteristics and qualities in your marriage? If so, describe them.

If you are not married, which would be the most important to you in a marriage relationship?

When you consider finding a mate and being a mate for life, which qualities mean the most to you?

2. Scan the Song of Solomon. What characteristics of this newly married couple's friendship stand out to you?

3. Sex in marriage was designed by God to draw a couple together. Why do you think it should deepen their friendship?

What influences in society cause the opposite of this to happen?

What are some ways a couple can avoid the erosion of their joy in this aspect of their marriage friendship?

4. What godly principles does I Corinthians 7 offer for safeguarding a marriage friendship strengthened through sex?

5. Read Song of Solomon 5:1-16. What hindered the friendship between Solomon and his bride?

How did the bride begin to enjoy their friendship again (5:10-16)?

When you're feeling out of sorts with your husband, how can thinking about his positive qualities help your relationship and your friendship?

6. How would applying the commands of Philippians 4:8 enhance your marriage friendship?

Is this difficult or easy to do? Why?

In what specific ways can you choose to apply each of these commands this week?

7. What truths or principles of marriage in the following Proverbs would help women strengthen the friendship in their marriage?

- Proverbs 12:4—

- Proverbs 14:1—

- Proverbs 15:17—

- Proverbs 19:13—

- Proverbs 19:14—

- Proverbs 21:9,19—

- Proverbs 27:15-16—

- Proverbs 31:10-12—

Which of these truths do you think your husband would most like you to apply?

8. Scan Genesis 3. Do you think Adam and Eve were friends as well as mates? Why?

How did temptation and difficult times affect their friendship?

Have difficult circumstances strengthened or diminished your friendship with your husband?

If your friendship has diminished, how can you respond to him in a way that will renew it?

9.
What one thing will you do this week to strengthen the friendship in your marriage?

If you are not married, what habits and character traits can you be forming now that will strengthen any friendship, including friendship in marriage?

My Precious Princess and Daughter—

No one, not even a husband, can fill your deepest longings and desires for intimacy and friendship—no one can but Me. But I do want to bless you with close friendships, and, if I lead you into a marriage, I want your husband to be the deepest and most intimate of all human friends. But I never want you to take your eyes off Me; I am the only One who can meet your deepest needs. It is unfair of you to expect that of any earthly friend, even a husband.

Your husband has a different perspective on life, but I designed you both . . . to complement each other. Instead of viewing him as an irritation, can you be grateful for the different perspective he offers? That is the way you will grow the closest, by valuing his perspective. Can you consider the importance of another person's ideas as My way to give you insight . . . and help? Don't you see? He is another of My gifts to you—a friend who will be strong when you are weak; encourage you when you are sad; stretch you to venture out of your comfort zone.

That doesn't mean you'll always get along perfectly, but My desire is for you to enjoy each other. Welcome his ideas as My gifts. If he is leading you astray in some way, I'll let you know and strengthen you to take a stand. But in most things, cherish the gift I've given you through the human friendship of marriage.

Your husband will never be able to love you perfectly, but I will always love you with an everlasting love.

Lovingly,
Your Heavenly Father, the King

Overcoming Competition

Does it seem like you are always in competition with someone? You may even be great friends, yet because of similar experiences, personalities, or challenges, you must fight against unhealthy feelings of competition. God knows friends can have that effect on each other. His Word tells us how to compete with competition between friends.

1. In what areas might friends struggle with competition?

Can competition between friends ever be healthy or good for the friendship? Explain.

Do you think certain kinds of personalities are more prone to competition? Which kinds and why?

What part might envy play in such feelings?

2. Read Genesis 29:1—30:25. What began the unhealthy competition between Rachel and Leah?

How do you think each of these people contributed to the feelings of competition in this situation?

Laban—

Jacob—

Rachel—

Leah—

How did God use both women (Ruth 4:11)? What does that say to you about the uselessness of competition or the benefit of working toward the same goals, united in a godly purpose?

3. Read Genesis 31:1-16. What common ground did Rachel and Leah find?

Why did it create harmony between them?

If two friends feel competitive toward each other, how could they apply James 4:5-7 to control their feelings?

4. What truths in James 3:13-18 could Christian friends apply to overcome any disharmony between them?

What does James 3:14 identify as possible sources of competition?

In contrast, how does God want friends to respond to each other (James 3:17-18)?

Why would Satan want to generate unhealthy competition between Christians?

5. How could the truth expressed in Philippians 1:27 help friends to resist competitive acts or feelings?

6. From these verses, how does God want friends to overcome feelings of competition between them?

- Proverbs 17:14—

- Romans 15:4-7—

- Galatians 6:2-5—

- Philippians 2:1-2—

- Philippians 2:3-4—

- Philippians 2:5-8—

Which of these truths is most difficult for you to apply in your life? Why?

Which is easiest to apply? Why?

7. State one practical way a friend might fulfill the exhortation of Philippians 2:5-8 (either you to a friend, or a friend to you).

8. How could the following verses from Proverbs bring greater harmony between competing friends?

- 17:9—

- 21:2-3—

- 29:23—

9. How could striving for contentment as described in Philippians 4:11-13 be a solution for competitive friends?

What insight(s) do you receive from Paul's perspective of contentment in those verses?

Why is that a godly perspective?

How will you apply that perspective to your life?

10. What godly advice would you give a friend who struggles with a competitive spirit toward a friend?

If you struggle with a competitive spirit toward coworkers, how could you change that attitude? Should you change it?

11. When you struggle in this area, what will you do to resist letting a competitive spirit mar your relationships based on the verses or principles covered in this study?

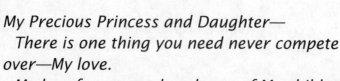

My Precious Princess and Daughter—

There is one thing you need never compete over—My love.

My love for you and each one of My children is so incredible and inexhaustible that there is more than enough for everyone. You don't ever need to feel insecure or wonder if I love one more than another. My intense affection and concern for you is never diminished by being shared. You cannot compete or work for My love. It is a gift.

Jacob couldn't give that kind of love to both Rachel and Leah, and so they began to compete for his love. Too many of My children think they have to fight each other to gain My attention or approval. They let themselves fall victim to the deceiver's lies and want to be perceived by the world as better than someone else. But I don't want you, My Daughter, to feel like that. I love each one of My children equally and completely. Come to Me and sit at My side. You are not in competition with anyone else for My approval or love.

If your friend seems to be competing with you in some way, let it be. Take on My Son's humble attitude. Allow her to "win." And be honest with her when you feel tempted to compete as well. You will be freed from thinking you have to always be right, always ahead, always in front. That isn't the way I want My children to think. Won't you seek to please Me? I will lift you up and hold you close. Trust Me. My way is always for your best. No one can ever come between us. I can never love anyone else more than you.

Lovingly,
Your Heavenly Father, the King

Times of Need

We all experience times of need, and it is in those times that friends are especially important. God has designed friendship as a source of strength and comfort for us. They bring us joy in the midst of trouble and allow us to bring joy to others when they are in need.

1. Describe a time of trial or difficulty when a friend was especially important to you.

How was your friend helpful or a blessing to you?

How have you been a help to a friend in a time of trouble?

2. Scan the book of Ruth. Have you ever experienced feelings similar to Naomi's?

How could a friend have helped you in such circumstances?

What kind of help did Ruth give to Naomi?

How can in-laws become friends, the kind of friends you can depend upon in times of trouble?

3. What do you like best about Ruth's response to Naomi in Ruth 1:16?

If you had been Ruth, what, if anything, would you have found frustrating as you dealt with a depressed person like Naomi?

How would you have handled that?

4. Since Ruth was of a different culture and religion originally, it seems that Naomi and her family had a deep, spiritual impact on her life (Ruth 1:4,16-17). Read Ruth 1:8-14. Do you think Orpah was less of a friend to Naomi than Ruth was? Explain.

Why can it seem easier to turn away in a friend's time of need?

Would it ever be best to turn away from a friend in need? Explain.

5. How does God bless Ruth's and Naomi's friendship (Ruth 4:13-17)?

6. How does Ruth's and Naomi's friendship illustrate the truth of Proverbs 17:17?

7. When trying to help a friend seems too overwhelming, of what does Galatians 6:9-10 remind us?

8. Galatians 6:2 and 6:5 seem to give conflicting messages in dealing with others. But they contain very good advice for helping those in need. Some burdens need to be carried and worked through by people—it would be unhealthy for someone else to carry all of their burdens for them. Other burdens are too much to bear or can be lightened by simple encouragement. Give an example of a time when it might be more harmful than helpful to carry someone else's burden.

What might God want us to learn from helping someone else?

What might God want us to learn about accepting help from others?

Give an example of a time when carrying another's burden would encourage or strengthen her.

9. What does God promise each of His children in our troubles (Matthew 11:28-30; Hebrews 4:16, 13:5)?

When you are trying to encourage a friend, how can you best point that person to Christ and His help?

10. What enables us to help others (Hebrews 10:22-23)?

11. What does God want us to encourage our friends to do?

- Hebrews 10:24—

- Hebrews 10:25—

12. What truths from the following verses does God want us to communicate when we are struggling?

- I Corinthians 10:13—

- I Peter 4:12-13—

- I Peter 4:15-16—

- I Peter 5:6-7—

- I Peter 5:10—

How could exhibiting confidence in these truths be a testimony of your faith in Christ?

13. What further truths or insights about times of trouble do these Proverbs verses give?

- 3:27-29—

- 14:32—

- 17:5—

- 20:5-6—

- 31:25-26—

14. Read Acts 18:24-28. What godly principles do you see in Priscilla's and Aquila's [ACK-wih-luh] actions for reaching out to people both to encourage and to correct?

15. As you've worked through this study, what has God brought to your heart about helping a hurting person? What action will you take this week?

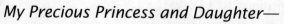

My Precious Princess and Daughter—

Life on earth can be very difficult. Illness, trials, stress, persecution, conflict, even growing old can cause many hearts to ache. Friendships are one of My ways for helping people see My love for them. I want to use you, My Beloved Daughter, to bring encouragement and joy to others in times of need.

Please remember that you cannot be everything to everyone. If you try to meet everyone's needs, you'll only create a lack in your own heart. If you offer too much help or rescue others from the consequences of their choices, you may interrupt the work I'm trying to do in their hearts. Trust Me as I work in them. At the right time, you'll have the right words to say and the courage to say them. At the right opportunity, you'll reach out to them with comfort and I will give you the strength you need.

I will also provide the encouragement you need during the trials I give to you. Don't rebuff others when they want to help you. They may be My messengers to you, offering the help you so desperately want.

Precious One, you are My ambassador. I am using you, and you will be rewarded. Be a Ruth to the Naomis I bring to you. Yet, guard your own heart so that you're not drained of your joy in Me. Make sure your love flows from My heart. I love your friend. I love you. You cannot control the response of others. You do your part—the rest is up to Me— and I am fully capable. I am holding you both in My strong hands, close to My heart.

Lovingly,
Your Heavenly Father, the King

Being Friends with Our Children

A mother's heart—and a grandmother's—longs for fellowship and friendship with her children and grandchildren. When her children are young, a mother must respond to them as a mother, but as children mature, an adult-to-adult friendship is possible. Are you cultivating the soil of your home and their hearts so such a friendship can take root and thrive?

1. What kind of relationship do you have with your mother and/or grandmother(s)?

What do (or did) you like best about your mother?

Your grandmother(s)?

2. What characteristics describe a good adult friendship between a mother and her grown children?

3. Mothers aren't usually "friends" with their children as the children are growing up. Do you think it is necessary to maintain some boundaries? Why?

What foundation are you laying now for a future friendship with your adult children?

4. Read Acts 16:1 and II Timothy 1:3-5. What background information do you know about this family?

What united Lois and Eunice (II Timothy 1:5)?

What impact do you think that had on Timothy as a child and as a young man?

5. What seems to characterize Timothy's life based on these verses?

- I Corinthians 16:10-11—

- I Timothy 4:12—

- I Timothy 4:14—

- I Timothy 4:15-16—

- II Timothy 1:6-8—

6. What character qualities do your children have?

What difficulties/challenges are they facing that could cause you to worry?

How can worrying create tension in a friendship with your children when they are young?

When they are grown?

What should replace worry in the life of a Christian mother (or grandmother)?

7. What do these verses tell you to do?

- Proverbs 3:5-6—

- Ephesians 6:18—

- Philippians 4:6-7—

8. Why do these commands offer encouragement?

What do you see God doing in your children's lives right now?

In your life?

When you are tempted to worry about your children, what do you think that says about your view of God?

How can you model trust in God to your children?

9. How do the truths in the following verses describe God and how does the central truth in each apply to trusting Him for your children?

Verse	Description of God	Application
I Chron. 29:11-12		
Psalm 103:11		
Jeremiah 33:3		
Matthew 7:7-12		
I John 3:21-22		

Which of God's characteristics are most meaningful to you as you think of Him working in the lives of your children? (Choose from the descriptions on the previous page or other verses you know.)

10. What do you think your role should be as you deal with your children at these stages of their lives? If you do not have children, think about what your role should be in relationship to your parents, especially as an adult child.

Young children—

Teenagers—

Young adults—

Mature adults—

11. As you think of your present relationship with your children or with your parents, what signs of friendship do you see?

With your children—

With your parents—

How can you deepen your friendship with your children?

.

Are there things you can do to develop and deepen your friendship with your parents?

With your in-laws?

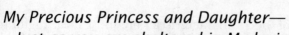

My Precious Princess and Daughter—

Just as you are sheltered in My loving, strong hands, your children are, too. I want you to have a wonderful friendship with them, and I will help you do that. Look for the things that show you I am working in mighty ways in their lives.

When you feel anxious and worried about them, stop—and trust Me. I know you want them to grow in their faith. Trust Me with them. As much as you love them, as much as you watch over them, I love them more and My power is more than sufficient to keep them safe.

No, I don't guarantee that nothing bad will happen to them, and I will not overrule all the choices they make, but I do guarantee that I will work everything together for their good. It may be painful for you to see them go through hard times, but trust Me even then. You can show them your concern, but it is your faith in Me that will draw them to you—and to Me.

My Beloved Child, relax! Know that I'm working. I am sovereign, trustworthy, gracious, merciful, patient, and kind. You cannot control or change your children no matter what their age may be, but you can pray for them. I will honor your prayers because you are My child and I love you.

Lovingly,
Your Heavenly Father, the King

Handling Conflict between Friends

o friendship is totally without conflict or misunderstandings. Working through these times bonds friends together—if we can just look at our differences positively. Often such situations are God's hand at work in our lives to mold us into Jesus' image, rubbing off the unpleasant corners of our personalities. Conflict is not always bad—and God can use it to bring more good than we imagine—if we handle it in Christlike love.

1. Do you think a true friendship should never have conflict? Explain your answer.

Give an example of a time you worked through a conflict in one of your friendships. Why did you make the effort?

2. Was there a time when conflict destroyed one of your friendships? What happened? Why did the friendship end?

When conflict destroys a friendship, what do you think is the main reason?

41

When a friendship withstands conflict, why do you think it survives?

3. Read Philippians 4:2-3 and Romans 12:18. What is our obligation before God when we have a conflict with a fellow believer?

4. How does each of these verses encourage harmony?

- Philippians 1:27

- Philippians 4:4

- Philippians 4:5

- Philippians 4:14

- Colossians 1:4-5

- Colossians 1:16-18

5. What seems to generate anger most often in your friendships?

From the verses on the following page, identify biblical principles for coping with anger, misunderstanding, or conflict.

<u>Verse</u>	<u>Principle</u>

- Ephesians 4:2

- Ephesians 4:3

- Ephesians 4:26-27

- Ephesians 4:29-30

- Ephesians 4:31

- Ephesians 4:32

6. What do these verses indicate are possible contributors to conflict in friendships?

- Proverbs 16:28—

- Proverbs 18:19—

- Titus 3:9—

7. Here are some guidelines for confronting a friend when such a step becomes necessary.

a—Pick a time and place convenient for the other person, with few distractions.

b—Have good motives; desire the best for the other person, not satisfaction for your hurt.

c—Pray about the time you will spend together and the words you will speak.

d—Give up expectations of a particular response.

e—Be willing to forgive.

f—Prepare what you'll say, write it out, practice it.

g—Be firm, but avoid name-calling or screaming.

h—Admit your own wrongdoing.

i—Stay on the issue; don't exaggerate or threaten.

j—Don't use absolute words like never, always, all the time, every day, constantly.

Which one of these is most difficult for you and which is easiest? Why?

8. Which of the guidelines above correlates with these verses? (They may not all be used.) What other guidelines do you see?

_____ Philippians 2:3
_____ Philippians 2:4
_____ Philippians 2:14
_____ Philippians 4:8
_____ Proverbs 15:1
_____ Proverbs 17:9
_____ Proverbs 18:13
_____ Proverbs 22:10
_____ Matthew 5:23-24
_____ Galatians 6:1
_____ Colossians 4:2,6
_____ I Thessalonians 5:14-15

9. Which of these verses and principles could help you in a current situation? How?

10. When it seems impossible to resolve a conflict between yourself and a friend, what godly principle does Philippians 3:13-15 give?

11. Ultimately, what is more important when faced with conflict? Trying to change someone's viewpoint, getting your own way, admitting your own part in the conflict, or...? (Consider I Corinthians 6:1-8 and Philippians 1:27.)

12. Why are conflicts between friends harmful?

When are conflicts between friends good?

13. Because of truths you have discovered in this study, what action(s) might God want you to take about any conflicts you may have with friends or family members?

My Precious Princess and Daughter—

Sadly, conflict, even between friends, is inevitable. But you are My representative, My child. I will empower you to respond in a godly manner. Whether problems arise with other members of My family or with those who don't know Me, I want you to treat them as I would.

Most of the time, the difficulties between friends erupt over minor issues, so why make a big deal out of such things? Remember how I hate pride? I exalt the humble, and if the issue is really that important, I will arrange a change of heart. If the issue is important enough for you to confront your friend and take a stand for righteousness, then plan carefully what you'll say. Seek My wisdom, and I will help you to face the issues in ways that honor Me. And if I continue to direct in that way, know that I will enable you to respond in a godly manner.

Beloved Child, I love you and your friend equally. I don't pick sides or have favorites. My real concern is for holiness and righteousness. For My sake, follow the commands in My Word and restore your friendship. I want My children to be unified in serving Me and in showing My love to the world. No relationship will be perfect until you join Me in Heaven, but seeking peace with others can give you a glimpse of the perfection that is to come. I want your best. I love you with an everlasting love. There is no conflict I cannot solve—if you'll relinquish your pride and seek My will in child-like humility.

Lovingly,
Your Heavenly Father, the King

Differing Personalities

From the first two people created by God—first from the dust of the earth and then a rib—to the baby born just this minute, God has made every human being different. We each look at life from our own unique perspective, and yet, He is the Creator of us all. What an infinitely ingenious God! Different isn't bad; many times it adds the spice that makes life so exciting.

1. There are many methods used to categorize different personalities or temperaments. Is there one that you have used or prefer? Why?

What basic personality traits have you observed in yourself?

In others close to you?

In your boss or coworkers?

What potential difficulties in friendships could these personality differences create?

What have you found helpful for limiting misunderstandings between people with different personalities?

2. Mary and Martha give us an example of different personalities and perspectives of life. Read the following passages and share your general observations about these two sisters' perspectives of life and Jesus.

Luke 10:38-42

John 11:1-44

John 12:1-3

3. Every personality type has positive and negative characteristics. Even a good character trait taken to extremes or used inappropriately can turn into a negative.

What are Mary's . . .
    . . . positive personality characteristics?

    . . . negative personality characteristics?

What are Martha's . . .
    . . . positive personality characteristics?

    . . . negative personality characteristics?

4. With which sister do you identify the most, Mary or Martha? Why?

What are your . . .
   . . . positive personality characteristics?

   . . . negative personality characteristics?

How can each of your personality traits be used positively, to benefit others?

5. What do your friends seem to like best about you?

What do your friends seem to dislike about you?

6. With which of your personality traits do you think you please the Lord the most? Why or how?

Do you think God gave you the negative traits? Why? Explain your answer.

How can you work on changing your negative traits to positive ones?

How do your personality characteristics affect the types of friends you seek or your choice of husband?

What positive personality traits does your husband have? If you aren't married, what traits would be important to you in a husband?

7. Read I Corinthians 12:12-27. What stands out to you about this passage?

How would these parts of the body be reflected in differing personalities?

8. Read I Corinthians 12:28-30. How do those verses support the need for differing personalities?

Using your imagination, what part of the Body of Christ are you, and how do you think God has designed your personality to fulfill your role? (Example: I'm a part of the inner ear because I help to bring balance to the body of Christ.)

9. How do the truths of I Corinthians 12:12-30 enable you to overcome any jealousy toward another member of the Body of Christ or that person's role in it? What about anger? A critical spirit?

10. Read I Corinthians 13. Among the characteristics of love named there, which one would help you accept a friend with a different personality?

11. Read Romans 14:1—15:1. Although this passage refers to those weak in faith, the same general principles could also be applied to those with differing viewpoints of life. What principles for dealing with friends with differing qualities do you find there?

12. Why do you think God brings people very different from us into our lives?

What have you found most helpful in this study for understanding and loving a friend who is different from you?

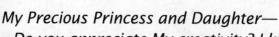

My Precious Princess and Daughter—

Do you appreciate My creativity? I know such diversity can be the source of great difficulties, but just think what problems might arise if everyone had similar personalities. The variety I created represents who I am and My immense power. Those differences are designed to create greater love and understanding between My family members.

My Daughter, you are a valued member in the Body of Christ, My Son's church. If you will appreciate the strengths of each of your brothers and sisters, your friendships will be strengthened. There won't be jealousy, competition, or judgment. When you each fulfill the plan I have, you grow in love for your fellow Christians.

That's when the world sees My children at their best—operating as a whole, seeking to honor Me. You're all on the same side! Look for reflections of Me in your Christian friends. See each one's unique personality as My stamp on their lives. And be gentle when you notice the marks of the world's influences in their lives.

Don't try to change them—instead, cooperate with the design I've created within them. Build them up; don't tear them down! Compliment their strengths and encourage them to overcome their weaknesses. Let your friendships draw the world closer to My loving arms.

I created you! I created your friend! Rejoice in the differences I gave you! I love you both!

Lovingly,
Your Heavenly Father, the King

Mentoring Friendships

We all need encouragement and advice at times. Friendships that also mentor us can meet that need. What mature women have experienced and learned should be passed on. But how do such friendships develop? God's Word gives us a plan.

1. What does a mentoring friendship mean to you? How would you describe it?

What are the advantages and disadvantages of a mentoring friendship?

What needs would be met by two friends in such a relationship?

2. The mature woman in a mentoring relationship is often referred to as the "Titus Woman." Look at Titus 2:3-5. From those verses, list the qualities and behaviors that an older woman should encourage in a younger woman.

How would you use each of those qualities or behaviors to mentor someone else?

Which of those qualities or behaviors is something you need to grow in?

3. How would you describe holy or reverent behavior (verse 3)?

Think of a woman at least 10 years older than you whom you would consider a good model or mentor. What are some examples of her attitudes or actions that make you think that?

4. If you were the more mature woman in a mentoring friendship, how would you encourage a younger woman to . . .

. . . love her husband?

. . . love her children?

. . . show love to a stranger?

5. How would you teach or express the principles of I Peter 3:1-6 to a younger woman?

6. Do you think mentoring can only happen between older women and younger women or could/should a younger woman mentor an older woman? Explain your answer.

What is necessary for someone to be able to mentor someone else, spiritually or socially?

7. What qualifications for a mentor do you see in II Corinthians 1:3-4?

What qualifications might II Peter 1:3-8 add to this picture?

Do you think a mentor would have to have all of these qualities? Explain your answer.

What qualities do you think would be most important?

8. What do the verses on the following page give as the principles and/or benefits of a mentoring relationship?

- Proverbs 11:14—

- Proverbs 11:16—

- Proverbs 12:1, 13:18—

- Proverbs 13:20—

- Proverbs 27:17—

9. From the following verses in Proverbs, name the qualities that you would look for in a mentor or offer as a mentor. When the verse describes the negative quality of someone you should avoid, record the opposite quality you should seek.

Proverbs Verses	Look For/Seek
3:31-32	
14:7	
16:28-29	
20:19	
22:24-25	
23:6-8	
23:9	
23:20-21	
24:3-4	
24:5-6	
25:11-12	
25:13	
25:19	

10. Mark the qualities in the list that characterize your life now. How are you using these to encourage your coworkers?

Your children?

Your husband/boyfriend?

Your best friend(s)?

11. In what areas of life would you want someone to mentor you?

Which of these positive qualities do you need in someone whom you would want to mentor you?

How would you ask a friend to mentor you?

12. Which two kinds of people are described in Proverbs 9:7-12?

What are the benefits of being the kind who learns?

What are the disadvantages of being the kind of person who refuses to learn?

My Precious Princess and Daughter—

Many women have already traveled the road that you are now traveling. Their experiences can help you. It doesn't matter how old or young a woman is, a woman of any age can be blessed by seeking the advice of another.

Such relationships need not be formally determined; they can happen spontaneously. But I want each of My precious daughters to be encouraged in their walk with Me. That isn't weakness; it demonstrates wisdom to seek out those who can hold you up in times of frailty, share your joy in times of encouragement, and challenge you in low times.

My Chosen One, I will direct you to one who will strengthen you. And you have something of value to share, too. I am working in your life! Reach out to those on a journey similar to yours. Describe the bumps that you've encountered both in the valleys and on the way to the mountaintops—and how you saw Me make the road passable, even smooth.

My Child, I love you and have designed you to need mentoring friendships. Don't be afraid to ask for a friend whose wisdom and guidance you can trust because she, too, walks closely with Me. I will provide the right person. And remember, I am your most valued Mentor, for I know what lies ahead, and My lovingkindness will give you guidance no other can provide.

Lovingly,
Your Heavenly Father, the King

The Ultimate Friendship

Nothing can take the place of friendship with God. He is the best Best Friend anyone can have. He is faithful and true, loving and kind. All other human friendships are only a hazy reflection of the friendship God offers to any who seek Him—and gives to all who receive Jesus Christ as Saviour.

1. How would you describe your friendship with God?

Why do you think God wants to have a close relationship with you?

How can you make it closer, deeper, richer?

2. Read John 4:1-42. What impresses you most about the interaction between Jesus and the Samaritan woman? What kind of friendship did Jesus offer the woman?

In what ways did the Samaritan woman resist Jesus' friendship? Why?

In what ways are you like the Samaritan woman as you respond to Jesus' desire to develop a friendship with you?

In what ways are you unlike the Samaritan woman?

3. How do the following verses reflect God's desire to have a friendship with His human creations?

- Romans 3:21-24—

- Romans 4:4-8—

- Romans 5:6-8—

- Hebrews 4:16—

- Hebrews 10:19-22—

4. Read Psalm 46:1-3,10. What does God offer us as His friends? Why?

A true friendship must be based on knowing someone intimately. Knowing the truth about God helps develop your friendship with Him. What do you think it means to know God intimately?

How would praying Psalm 86:11 deepen your relationship with God?

5. From the following verses, describe the nature of God.

- Exodus 20:5—

- Deuteronomy 32:4—

- Psalm 25:8-9—

- Psalm 86:15—

- Psalm 147:5—

- Malachi 3:6—

- Matthew 11:29-30—

- Romans 11:33—

- I John 4:8-10—

Which of those qualities is most important to you?

How would you describe your nature? How is it different from God's? How is it similar?

6. Pick one attribute and describe a time when God showed Himself to you by that attribute.

7. If a person believes a lie about God's character, how could that hamper a friendship with Him?

Have you ever misunderstood something about God and then realized the truth? Explain.

What difference did that make in your friendship with Him?

8. Why do friendships take time and effort?

The following verses give ingredients for developing a relationship with God. For each verse, list the ingredient and why you think each is important.

* Joshua 1:8

* Psalm 150:1

* II Corinthians 9:6-9

* I Thessalonians 5:17

* I Thessalonians 5:18

* Hebrews 10:25

* I John 1:9

9. Do you want to have a deeper friendship with God? If so, how will you cultivate it and deepen your relationship?

As you look back over the elements of friendship with God, state one specific goal you will pursue this coming week to develop that friendship.

How do you anticipate that your relationship and friendship with God will deepen or change as a result? How will you know that it is changing?

Is there someone you could ask to keep you accountable for your goal? Ask that person to help you by 6:00 p.m. tomorrow.

10. Read John 3:3. Why is being "born again" the only way we can begin a friendship with God?

If you've never been born again and would like to begin a friendship with God, you can pray this or a similar prayer:

"Heavenly Father, thank you for loving me so much that you sent your Son, Jesus, to die in my place on the cross, as a sacrifice for my sins. I want to trust in Jesus as my Saviour and receive eternal life. I believe that He is Your Son and that You raised Him from the dead. I know I am a sinner. Please forgive me of my sin, cleanse me, and make me Your precious daughter, a princess. Thank You for saving me. I pray this in Jesus' name. Amen."

My Precious Princess and Daughter—

I'm thrilled that you want to deepen our friendship. There is nothing I want more than for you to know Me intimately. It grieves Me deeply when we aren't in close fellowship.

The depth and closeness of our friendship is your protection against doubt and lies about Me. Our adversary, the devil, eagerly spreads lies about Me. I know how hard it can be for you to trust Me and to seek My attention, but there is nothing you need fear. I know you intimately and I love you completely—no matter what. Please trust My great love for you. Seek Me. Know Me. I want to pour My lavish love over your heart and soul so that you will rejoice in knowing Me and hunger to know Me more.

From the beginning of time I have had you in mind. I sent Jesus to die for you so that we could be reconciled and have this close friendship. It was a terrible price—but He paid it willingly. Only your sin prevented you from knowing My wonderful love. Jesus' blood, shed for you on the cross, blotted out your sin and made our friendship possible the moment you believed and received My Son Jesus as your Saviour.

So come to Me boldly. The door to My throne room is always open and the welcome mat is always out! You are My precious daughter and although there is sin in your life, absolutely nothing need keep you from turning back to Me for forgiveness. Keep looking forward to that day when you'll enter My presence in heaven and we'll be together forever!

Lovingly,
Your Heavenly Father, the King